The Moth

Paul Herzberg

methuen | drama

LONDON • NEW YORK • OXFORD • NEW DELHI • SYDNEY

METHUEN DRAMA

Bloomsbury Publishing Plc, 50 Bedford Square, London, WC1B 3DP, UK
Bloomsbury Publishing Inc, 1385 Broadway, New York, NY 10018, USA
Bloomsbury Publishing Ireland, 29 Earlsfort Terrace, Dublin 2,
D02 AY28, Ireland

BLOOMSBURY, METHUEN DRAMA and the Methuen
Drama logo are trademarks of Bloomsbury Publishing Plc.

First published in Great Britain 2025

Cover design by Anita Clipston | www.anitaclipston.com

Bloomsbury Publishing Plc does not have any control over, or responsibility
for, any third-party websites referred to or in this book. All internet addresses
given in this book were correct at the time of going to press. The author and
publisher regret any inconvenience caused if addresses have changed or sites
have ceased to exist, but can accept no responsibility for any such changes.

No rights in incidental music or songs contained in the work are hereby
granted and performance rights for any performance/presentation
whatsoever must be obtained from the respective copyright owners.

All rights whatsoever in this play are strictly reserved and application
for performance etc. should be made before rehearsals begin to Blake
Friedmann Literary Agency Ltd, Ground Floor, 15 Highbury Place, London,
N5 1QP. No performance may be given unless a licence has been obtained.

A catalogue record for this book is available from the British Library.

Library of Congress Control Number: 2025932404

ISBN: PB: 978-1-3505-6066-6
ePDF: 978-1-3505-6067-3
eBook: 978-1-3505-6068-0

Series: Modern Plays

Typeset by Mark Heslington Ltd, Scarborough, North Yorkshire

For product safety related questions contact
productsafety@bloomsbury.com.

To find out more about our authors and books visit
www.bloomsbury.com and sign up for our newsletters.

THE MOTH

by

Paul Herzberg

For Oona

With special thanks to:

Jake Murray and Elysium Theatre Company, Chris Neville-Smith,
David Clough, John Washbrook, Julian Friedmann

The Moth was first commissioned for YouTube as part of the Covid-19 Monologues.

It won the Olwyn Wymark Award for Elysium Theatre Company, best monologue at The Kwanzaa Film Festival NYC, and was chosen for 26 international film festivals:

CONTENTS

PREFACE

The Angolan Border War

I left South Africa at the age of twenty-three, having just returned from the Angolan Border War as a re-conscripted soldier. It was 1976. Five years earlier I had completed National Service. In the intervening period things had changed. South Africa was caught in a volatile period, much happening on its borders and within. Black Consciousness was exploding in the townships, the Portuguese had fled Angola and Soweto was in flames.

The war in which I had been involved was like no other. It was entirely secret. Soldiers were forced to pledge their silence to the Apartheid regime, who were desperate that word did not get out internationally as to what was going on beyond the Namibian border. It is a silence many maintain to this day. Parts of that war were so harrowing that thousands of ex-soldiers on both sides still suffer from post-traumatic stress disorder.

Angola borders Namibia, then, under occupation by South Africa, with its own liberation movement, SWAPO, in exile, operating from wherever it could: chiefly southern Angola. The white regime, fearing repercussions of a newly elected Marxist government in Angola and burgeoning Russian, Chinese and Cuban influence in the region, mustered 100,000 national service and civilian force soldiers to the border. At the same time, thousands of Cuban soldiers gathered to the north, uniting with local MPLA Angolan and SWAPO forces.

Hundreds of hot pursuit attacks were launched across the border into Angola. The first major strike, 'Operation Savannah' and brought the South Africans within twenty kilometres of Luanda, Angola's capitol city. Over the next thirteen years, thousands of Angolans and Namibians were slaughtered and many white and black South African troops. It was South Africa's Vietnam and involved the superpowers, exerting covert influence. A grim legacy of that war is that Angola remains the most mine-ridden country in the world.

The battle of Cuito Cuanavale in 1989 proved to be a major turning point and was the largest in Africa since the Second World War. The Angolan forces, boosted in numbers, hardware and military tactics by the Cubans, finally held their ground. While both sides claimed victory, within months, negotiations for Nelson Mandela's release began, as did the groundwork for the dismantling of Apartheid.

Refugees and migrants from South Africa to the United Kingdom

Between 1948, when the white Nationalist government came into power in South Africa, and the present day, there have been several waves of South Africans coming to live in, or flee to, the United Kingdom. Each has been characterised by developing events in the home country. When the ANC was banned after the Sharpeville massacre in 1960, for example, many people in the liberation movement fled. The diaspora was substantial: some went to Eastern Europe where they were welcomed by a variety of communist regimes; others fled to various parts of Africa, like Zambia and Tanzania, and a significant portion came to the United Kingdom. The anti-Apartheid movement flourished in London, led, inter alia, by Peter Hain and Oliver Tambo. Other waves included young men refusing to serve in the SADF, or those, like the writer, who chose to no longer be available to the Apartheid army or live in a country where racial oppression was sanctioned by the state.

The three scripts that led to *The Moth*

This is my fourth script exploring, in part, the South African military experience. In each case my aim was to make the themes universal in nature.

Sweet Like Suga, the first, was set in Angola, and directed by our co-producer on *The Moth*, Andy Jordan, for Bristol

Express. It was also produced in Canada at the Centaur Theatre, Montreal and Theatre 2000, Ottawa.

Two conscripted white soldiers, a rural Afrikaner and a pot-smoking English-speaking South African, at loggerheads, find themselves lost in the Angolan Bush. Out of nowhere, a mixed-race soldier in SADF uniform appears, Suga Peters, and offers to guide them back to the border. The interaction between the three men proves to be explosive as they attempt to grapple with the terrain and their inner demons – and for the two white soldiers, there is mounting suspicion of their enigmatic guide – all informing an apocalyptic ending.

The Song of My Father, also directed by Andy Jordan, was a sixty-minute play for BBC Radio 4, that starred Michael Maloney. Private Ray Kemp is the marching puppet of his retired NCO father. Ray's squad has been chosen to represent his unit at the national marching competition in Pretoria. Corporal Kruger, NCO in charge of their training, is a brutal instructor who delights in driving his squad to the brink.

Ray tries to protect a vulnerable recruit in the squad, Clive Mendelowitz, from Kruger's cruelty, but incurs the wrath of his father for allowing himself to be distracted. Clive eventually takes his own life, which alters Ray irrevocably, and he sabotages his squad's drill offering at the competition, to his father's horror. Twenty years later, Ray, now an exile in London, bumps into Kruger on a train and confronts him about the past.

The Dead Wait was nominated for the Verity Bargate Award and was first produced at the Market Theatre, South Africa, in 1997. It was adapted for radio and produced by the BBC, ABC Australia and WDR, Germany. It is currently under option in its adapted screenplay form. In 2002, it received its UK premiere at the Royal Exchange, directed by Jake Murray. The production was nominated for three Manchester Evening News awards, including best play and best production, winning in the category of best actor, for Oliver Dimsdale. It was produced at the Park Theatre in 2013, in an updated version, directed by Joe Harmston and re-published by Oberon Books.

At the age of thirty-nine I began a conversation with a man on a train in the UK. Intrigued by my background he told me of an incident that had befallen his nephew as a young soldier in the border war. He had been on an Angolan mission and his unit had captured a wounded black freedom fighter. The unit commander had it in for the young soldier and suspecting their captive might be important, ordered the soldier to carry him on his back until they reached the border for interrogation. The freedom fighter whispered into the soldier's ear as they moved through the bush – and in the mayhem, a bond began to grow. The commander, maddened by this unexpected course of events, finally responded to their unlikely friendship and ordered the soldier to execute the freedom fighter. This image, one man on the back of another in the bush, ally and foe locked together, haunted me. Using my long absence from the country, I found a way to build a play round the anecdote, to connect it to contemporary South Africa.

The Moth

After *The Dead Wait*, I felt that I had explored this period of history enough. Then, during Covid lockdown, Jake Murray approached me and said that he was producing a series of short monologues for YouTube as a way of staying in touch with theatre. He asked if me I had anything. I did – a partly written monologue that emerged from my discussions with former conscript, Angolan war veteran, film director and writer, Marius van Niekerk, during research for the film of *The Dead Wait*.

Marius told me several harrowing stories about that war. I used detail from some of them. One in particular, stayed with me, but there had been no place for it in the adapted screenplay: about a young white conscript battling PTSD, ordered to stand guard over a fatally wounded black freedom fighter, how the traumatised conscript had responded to the agony of his ward, and how he was deeply affected by the consequences: a strange hiss escaping from the captive's body after he took his last breath, and how, in the febrile mind of the conscript, it was as if the dead man's soul was flowing into him. In responding to this extraordinary anecdote, I reimagined that escaping soul as a moth flying into the night sky – and the haunting sound of tiny, beating wings.

Again, I started to build a broader narrative to that story. Given my fifty-year absence from South Africa, and issues surrounding race and racism which are once again front and centre of global politics, it seemed that this anecdote offered a fresh perspective on some pressing subjects.

Initially, this took the form of a twelve-minute monologue, called *The Moth*, acted brilliantly by Victor Power on YouTube, directed by Jake for Elysium. The format was simple. A static camera focused on the face of the narrator, who recalled an incident on a train when an ex-soldier confessed something harrowing to him, how it altered his life and how, in telling us, that anecdote can never be forgotten.

Jake and I were astonished when it found its way into twenty-six separate film festivals as a short, won the Olwyn Wymark Award for Elysium and the best monologue at The Kwanzaa Film Festival in New York, gaining, to date, nearly 6,000 views.

The next step seemed clear – surely there was a full-length play to be written, drawn for the monologue?

I am deeply grateful to Jake Murray, who was a boy of nine years old when I began working as a young actor and found myself frequently at the Royal Exchange, where his remarkable father, Braham, was one of the three artistic directors who had helped establish that theatre. It is my fifth collaboration with Jake, which has included playing Capulet at The Exchange, his masterly direction of *The Dead Wait* there, my brief offering on his tour of *The Island*, playing the lead in a play by August Strindberg at Jermyn Street, and now, *The Moth*.

There is someone who I must also mention: my wife, Oona. Her remarkable patience and rapier-sharp sense of story have been of great importance to me as a writer.

THE MOTH

The play is set in the United Kingdom and covers twenty-eight years. The two men are in their late twenties when they meet.

While the set can be limited to one neon sign with the word, 'Confessional' (lit during the monologues), two train seats and a carriage table, the images on the screen/train window and pre-recorded characters should present a clear, changing world.

John Josana	A British journalist
Marius Muller	A South African ex-special forces soldier
Train Guard	(Voice only)
DDR Border Guard	(Voice only)
Joy Josana	(Voice and image only)

ELYSIUM THEATRE COMPANY

Elysium Theatre Company (also known as Elysium Creative Arts) is an award-winning theatre company based in Durham. It was founded in 2017 by Jake Murray, Danny Solomon and Hannah Ellis Ryan. The goal was to produce small scale theatre in the North, eight years on our work is touring all across the region, from Newcastle, York and Leeds in the east to Manchester, Lancaster and Liverpool in the west. We have a strong commitment to drama that treats powerful themes, whether personal or private, psychological or social, in a dynamic, exciting and compelling way.

Our stage work includes a mixture of modern and period classics and, more recently, new writing. Notable productions include the regional premieres of *Jesus Hopped the a Train* by Stephen Adly Giurgis and *The River* by Jez Butterworth; Manchester and North East premieres of *Days of Wine and Roses* by Owen MacCafferty; significant revivals of works by Samuel Beckett, *Miss Julie* by August Strindberg and *A Doll's House* by Henrik Ibsen; the Fugard Trilogy – *Playland, Hello and Goodbye* and the 50th anniversary of *The Island*; and the world premiere of Steve Byron's *Reiver – Tales From The Borders*. In 2023 we launched the Durham Shakespeare Festival with *Macbeth* and *A Midsummer Night's Dream*. Last year we did the same with our touring production of *Othello*, which played in nineteen venues across the North.

We have a strong online presence. Our award-winning Covid-19 Monologues, all commissioned, rehearsed and filmed under lockdown conditions, won several awards. Our *Reiver – Voices From The Borders* initiative saw us explore the medium of audioplays, with three new instalments coming out later in the year. Our educational resources, from our exhaustive profiles of the world's greatest dramatists and the Shakespeare podcasts with some of the finest actors in our country, cover everything from North East history to Apartheid, all free to access.

We work on an ensemble basis, building up a company of actors whose work we admire and are interested in creating theatre with goals in common. We are incredibly proud to be bringing *The Moth* to twenty-five venues this spring.

THE COVID-19 MONOLOGUES

The Covid-19 Monologues were a new writing initiative Elysium developed during the global pandemic of 2020–22. When lockdown began in the UK, like all other theatre companies in the country Elysium's work was stopped in its tracks. We had a tour of *Look Back in Anger* planned for the spring which had to be cancelled. We had no idea what our future was going to be.

Inspired by an American friend, Anand Vyas (sadly no longer with us) who livestreamed footage of him playing his sitar to boost people's morale, AD Jake Murray hit upon the idea of the Covid-19 Monologues. These were micro-commissions designed to be rehearsed, filmed and released under lockdown conditions. Five writers were asked to write a short monologue each. The guidelines were simple: it had to be set in an interior location which meant it could be filmed safely, it would be filmed in one take with a static camera and could be about any subject. It could mention Covid or not.

The Moth was one of these first five. To our surprise, the whole series became so popular that we commissioned another five and then another five as we started to transition into the post-lockdown world. They included work from a cross section of British society – LGBT+, Jewish, Muslim, Afro-Caribbean, Malay; eleven were by Northern writers, six of which were based or set in the North East. They won multiple awards, including a prestigious Olwen Wymark Award from the Writers' Guild of Great Britain.

The Moth was selected for twenty-six film festivals across the world, from South Korea to Brazil, the UK and, of course, South Africa, and won Best Monologue at the Kwanzaa Film Festival in Harlem in NYC. It is the second of the monologues to be adapted and toured for the stage, the first being Steve Byron's *Blackmail* which became *Reiver – Tales From The Borders*. A third, *Fake* by Chris Barlas, has been also been adapted under the title *Truth* and awaits production.

'The Covid-19 Monologues' are available to watch on YouTube.

ELYSIUM ENGAGEMENT

Since 2020 Elysium's theatre work has been supported by a robust schools, higher education and communities engagement policy. Led by Ben Cain and Amy Mitchell, this seeks to enlarge the impact and access of our work as widely as possible among grass roots communities. We believe theatre has the power to change lives, and young people in particular should be able to see and take part in theatre whatever their backgrounds.

We have provided post-show discussions, Q&As and interactive workshops for productions such as *A Doll's House* and *The Island*. Our deep engagement scheme *Reiver – Voices From The Borders*, funded by Durham University, the National Lottery Heritage Scheme and Northumberland County Council, saw us work with six schools and youth groups across County Durham and Northumberland on creative response pieces reacting to a programme of workshops on the Reivers, and included three audioplays written by members of the general public.

Spurred on by an RSC/government report that discovered that children who saw live performances of Shakespeare outperformed those who didn't 90% of the time at GCSE and A level, we launched our our most ambitious initiative, Shakespeare For All in 2024. This takes Shakespeare into schools with workshops, Q&As and other events. Supported by the Arts Council, the John Thaw Foundation, No More Nowt and North East BIC, we were also able to provide free and discount tickets and travel to schools and children from socioeconomically deprived backgrounds to see our tour of *Othello* last year. That production attracted thirty-six schools and youth group parties alone.

We work closely with Durham University and Education Durham DCC on all our Engagement work. On *The Moth* we are proud to be collaborating with the Anti-Apartheid Legacy Centre and Archive, and Show Racism the Red Card to promote the play's message of an end to racial conflict.

To find out more about our Engagement work, see:

https://elysiumtc.co.uk/engagement/

Elysium Theatre Company presents:
The world premiere of

THE MOTH By Paul Herzberg

The time: Now
The place: Great Britain

CAST (in order of speaking):
John Josana – Faz Singhateh

Marius Muller – Micky Cochrane

Voice of Railway Announcer – Alexander Arran Cowan
Voice of DDR Security Guard – Paul Herzberg
Voice of Joy – Adjoa Andoh

First performed at the Queen's Hall Arts Centre Studio, Hexham
27 February 2025

CREATIVE AND PRODUCTION TEAM:

Director – Jake Murray
Producers – Jake Murray and Hannah Ellis Ryan
Consultant producer – Andy Jordan
Set and costume design – Amelia Mitchell
Lighting designer – Simon Cole
Sound and music – Paul G Clark
Projections and film designers – Paul G Clark and Amelia Mitchell
Production manager – Mark Turner
Stage manager – Rosie Fulton
Accent coach – Graham Eaglesham
Assistant directors – Matthew Travis and Raish Holloway
Engagement officer – Ben Cain
Poster designer – Anita Clipston
PR – Jake Rusby (Rusby Media) and Rachel Furst
Historical advisor – Rachel Johnson
Military advisor – Dr Brian Powers

With thanks to:
Rachael Barnwell, Damian Carr, Gez Casey, Lucy Curry,
Catharine Harwood, Caroline Kamara, Chris Neville-Smith, Katy
Taylor.

The Anti-Apartheid Legacy Centre and Archive, Education Durham, Durham University, Show Racism the Red Card, the Stanley Education Centre, Queen's Hall Arts Centre, Hexham.

With special thanks to:
The Anti-Apartheid Legacy Centre Archive, Jillian Edelstein and Tony and Gina Figueria for access to photography for projections.

SUPPORTED BY THE ARTS COUNCIL OF ENGLAND

Ben Cain – Engagement Officer

Ben attended the University of Hull, graduating in 2014 with a degree in Drama and Theatre Practice.

As a theatre practitioner and arts facilitator, Ben has worked with multiple arts organisations across the midlands and the north of England, including Richmond's Georgian Theatre Royal, Hull Truck Theatre, York Theatre Royal, Birmingham Repertory Theatre, Oldham Coliseum Theatre, M6 Theatre, Octagon Theatre Bolton and Factory International.

As part of Elysium's Engagement team, he has delivered creative projects on *A Doll's House* (2022), *The Island* (2023), the Durham Shakespeare Festival (2023) and *Othello* (2024), as well as co-developing Shakespeare For All, Elysium's flagship engagement programme, bringing accessible Shakespeare-focused creative opportunities to participants across County Durham and the North of England.

Paul G Clark – Sound, Music, Projections and Film Designer

Paul G Clark is a versatile musician based in the North East whose work blends pop, rock, blues, electronica and classical music. He has a first-class honours degree in Music and Sound, and a master's in Music.

Paul's extensive work includes sound design and composition for Elysium's *A Doll's House*, the *Reiver – Voices From The Borders* audio plays and all their online educational resource work – where his innovative approach to sound has left a lasting impact.

Other work includes the score of the short film The Visit produced by Mancmade scored, edit and sound design for audio play Penny Black's *Between Two Worlds*, based on the memoir by Maggie La Tourelle for Peracals Production, featuring Juliet Stevenson and Jane Lapotaire.

Micky Cochrane – Marius Muller

Micky Cochrane is an accomplished actor, singer and stand-up comedian based in the North East.

His work with Elysium includes Steve Byron's *Blackmail*: one of the original Covid Monologues which became *Reiver – Tales From The Borders* and toured the North East, and John Croser in the audio play *End Game* by Chris Neville-Smith as part of *Reiver – Voices From The Borders*.

Other work includes *I, Daniel Blake* (Tiny Dragon, Northern Stage and UK tour), *Billy Elliot* (Curve, Leicester), *The Pitmen Painters* (Oldham Coliseum), *Floorboards* (OddManOut, Alphabetti), and *A Nightingale Sang* (Live Theatre). He most recently appeared as Bill Muckle in *The Cramlington Train Wreckers* and will reprise his role of Glenn McCrory in the amazing true story *Carrying David* – taking to the stage of Newcastle Theatre Royal in June 2025 having toured in the North East, London and Northern Ireland to standing ovations and five-star reviews. Both were written by Ed Waugh.

TV and film credits include: *George Gently*, *The Dumping Ground*, and *Man Down* with Greg Davies.

Simon Cole – Lighting Designer

Si Cole is a lighting and video designer based in and from Teesside.

He works across multiple art forms – designing for theatre and dance and creating work with light, video and projection for intimate projects, contemporary art installations and outdoor events. He collaborates on immersive experiences that captivate audiences and push the boundaries of visual storytelling.

Recent theatre credits include: *A Song For Ella Grey* (Pilot Theatre), *The Watch House* (Papatango Theatre Company), *Penguin* (Curious Monkey Theatre), *Tiny Fragments of Beautiful Light* (Alphabetti Theatre), *Worlds Apart* (Woven Nest Theatre), *Fat Chance* (Rachel Stockdale), *Skybound* (TimbaDash Theatre), *All White Everything But Me* (Alphabetti Theatre), *Here* (Curious Monkey Theatre).

Rosie Fulton – Stage Manager

Rosie has worked in numerous touring stage management roles since completing her Stage Management (BA Hons) degree from the Royal Birmingham Conservatoire in 2021, where a show was taken on tour to Serbia sparking her passion for touring. During her time at university, Rosie discovered Elysium Theatre Company and has worked with them on several shows since graduating. A highlight of working with Elysium Theatre Company for Rosie has been working on shows such as *Reiver – Tales From The Border*, teaching some of the North East's history, and *The Island*, which tackled the subject of Apartheid. Rosie is excited to be back working with Elysium on *The Moth*.

Other credits for Rosie include the UK premiere of *Bloody Bloody Andrew Jackson*, *A Viking Christmas* and being part of the planning team for three seasons totalling almost thirty music festivals including Kubix, Monument and Lindisfarne.

Paul Herzberg – Writer

Paul cut his teeth as an actor at South Africa's first multi-racial theatre, *The Space*. He left for the UK in 1976 following conscription into the Angolan border war, a time he's drawn on for *The Song Of My Father* (BBC Radio 4), *Sweet Like Suga* (Old Red Lion & Centaur Montreal), his award-winning play, *The Dead Wait*, and more recently, *The Moth*. Paul completed a post-graduate diploma at LAMDA and began working as an actor and writer in the UK in 1978.

His work as a writer began on BBC Radio. It encompasses theatre, TV and film with several nominations and awards including The Nashville International Best Feature for *Almost Heaven* in which he plays the role of Blagden. *The Dead Wait* in which Paul played Papa Louw was produced at the Market Theatre, Royal Exchange and Park Theatre and was adapted for BBC Radio 4, ABC Australia, and WDR Germany. The play was shortlisted for The Verity Bargate Award and nominated for 3 Manchester Evening News Awards: best play, production and actor – in which category it won. In 2000 Paul was one of two writers commissioned for *The Metropolis Kabarett* at The National Theatre.

His screenplay for Ecosse, *Anna's Story*, won a place on the Brit List in 2018. His commissioned monologue for Elysium on You Tube, *The Moth*, was selected for 26 international film festivals, won the Olwyn Wymark Award and best monologue at The Kwanzaa Film Festival, New York.

Film and TV includes Daniel Borgoraz in the award-winning *The Honourable Woman*; Zava Zand in *Black Earth Rising*; Pattison QC in *Eastenders*; *Cry Freedom*; *The Life And Loves Of A She Devil*; *Smiley's People*; *Silo* and *The Teacher*, which was recently longlisted for a BAFTA Award.

Theatre includes Stanley Kowalski in *A Streetcar Named Desire* at the Mermaid; Gerry Evans in the world premiere of *Dancing At Lughnasa* at the Abbey; Gratiano in *The Merchant Of Venice* at Chichester with Alec Guinness as Shylock (Paul played Shylock at the Arcola); Vorster in Tony Sher's *I.D.* at the Almeida. He was at the RSC for *Taming Of The Shrew* and the National for *The Doctor's Dilemma* and the stage hit *Oslo*, which transferred to the Pinter Theatre.

Andy Jordan – Consultant Producer

Andy is a multi-award-winning producer, director and dramaturg in theatre, radio and online drama, specialising in new writing. He is also a sound artist, whose recent exhibits were at the Barbican Gallery and the Ashmoleon

Museum, Oxford. He has directed and produced plays in theatres across the UK, and in New York, Paris, Warsaw, Hong Kong and San Francisco, and has presented over thirty seasons of shows at the Edinburgh Fringe Festival. He was a Senior BBC radio drama producer for twelve years. He is the founder of Andy Jordan Productions Ltd, for whom he has produced/directed fifty-two productions.

Amelia Mitchell – Set, Costume and Projections Designer

Amelia Mitchell is a set designer with experience designing and creating props, sets and scenic art as well as skills within digital techniques. She has a BA degree in Production Design for Stage and Screen from the Northern School of Art and a MA in Design from the University of Sunderland.

Amelia has recently worked on the props for Niltoni Creatives' *Frankenstein*, and previous credits on *Sleeping Beauty* and *The Addams Family* at the Customs House. Amelia has gained work experience in prop creation for BBC comedy *Smoggie Queens*.

Jake Murray

Jake Murray is co-founder and artistic director of Elysium Theatre Company and has directed all but one of its plays. He directed all but one of the fifteen Covid-19 Monologues and all three of the *Reiver – Voices From The Borders* audioplays.

Jake has won numerous awards over the thirty years of his directing and has worked in theatres all over the country, including the London and Edinburgh Fringes, the Wolsey Theatre, Ipswich, the Chichester Festival Theatre and the Royal Exchange Theatre, Manchester. He has directed British premieres of plays by Brad Fraser, Tom Murphy, David Williamson, Janet Plater, Amy Rosenthal and Owen MacCafferty. Notable productions include *Romeo and Juliet* with Andrew Garfield and Gugu Mbatha-Raw as leads at the Royal Exchange and *A Whistle In The Dark* by Tom Murphy which transferred from the Royal Exchange to the Tricycle Theatre in London.

Most recently he has directed sold out site specific productions of *Frankenstein* and *A Christmas Carol* for Niltoni Creations in Newcastle. He also directed award-winning short film *The Visit* by Paul Ludden for Mancmade, starring Cal MacAninch.

Hannah Ellis Ryan – Producer

Hannah is an actor, writer and producer originally from Australia. She has been living in the UK since 2012, based in Manchester.

As an actor, Hannah has worked consistently across theatre and TV; most notably playing villain Hannah Gilmore in ITV's *Coronation Street* (thirty-plus episodes) and more recently starred in the TV adaptation of *Boiling Point*.

Hannah has her own theatre company HER Productions, who stage annual all-female Shakespeare productions across the North of England, as well as new writing and established plays. Their 2024 adaptation of *The Taming of the Shrew* was listed in The Stage's Top 50 Shows of 2024. In 2024 Hannah was also awarded the Olwyn Wymark Award for development in theatre from the Writers' Guild.

A co-founder of Elysium, Hannah co-produces their vast North Eastern tours and has played Lady Macbeth, Titania and Desdemona in *Macbeth*, *A Midsummer Night's Dream* and *Othello* respectively, Nora in *A Doll's House*, Hester in *Hello and Goodbye* and The Woman in *The River* in their productions.

Faz Singhateh – John Josana

Faz Singhateh trained at Guildhall School of Speech and Drama. For Elysium he has played Lucius Jenkins in *Jesus*

Hopped the A Train, Martinus Zoeloe in *Playland* and the title role in in Shakespeare's *Othello*.

Faz has appeared in the West End in *The Night of the Iguana* with Clive Owen and Lia Williams, *ear for eye* at the Royal Court, written and directed by debbie tucker green, Cornwall in Nancy Meckler's production of *King Lear* at The Globe and Assegai in *Raisin in the Sun* at the Young Vic. He played Tybalt in *Romeo and Juliet* and Strike in *On My Birthday* at the Royal Exchange Theatre, Manchester.

Screen work includes *Coronation Street*, *Waterloo Road*, *Hollyoaks* and *Emmerdale*. He is looking forward to presenting this world premiere of *The Moth*.

Mark Turner – Production Manager

Mark is a freelance lighting designer and production manager.

He has worked in the technical theatre industry since he was – when he first lit the musical Grease at high school. After graduating from Northumbria University in 2013 he worked for six years on cruise ships, from rigger on Cirque and lighting technician to technical manager on the Celebrity Fleet, as well as a freelance technician for various events companies and theatres in the UK between contracts.

Once the cruise ship life came to an end, Mark founded BrightStar, his own company providing hire equipment and technicians for touring shows, festivals, events and weddings. During the summer he freelances as production manager and lighting designer on festivals across the country, and in winters on pantomimes. For a number of years he has worked for Crossroads Entertainement (Then QDOS Pantomimes) and on The TwinsFX installing illusions and large special effects and flying systems into pantomimes across the country.

Since 2019 he has been production manager and lighting designer for Elysium productions such as *Miss Julie*, *The Island* and *The Moth*.

The Moth

Act One

Scene One

Blackness.

A sound: the flutter of tiny wings, ominous. It swells and swells.

The sound cuts dead.

In the blackness, a dimly lit red-neon sign flickers on, with one word: 'confessional'.

John *in a spot.*

He talks to us.

John You think you know me. You don't. – So, it's time to talk.

On screen: **John** *as a baby, held by his father,* **George**, *at a bleak African checkpoint.*

Caption: Zambia / Tanzania border, 1976.

John I was in prison the day I was born. It thrilled me. Scared me. But offered an anchor growing up as a kid, given who I was. Who I am. Black. The son of a refugee. A refugee whose identity is wrapped in story. So – many – damn – stories. A kind of a prison.

Pause.

Racism was clear in the eighties. In plain sight. A sneer; a smirk, the edge to a slight. Or just plain in-yer-face bile, 'FUCK OFF BLACK BASTARD!'

Pause.

Yup.

Pause.

Now? It's insidious. Subtle. There's this shiny new surface. Of piety. Tight-lipped support. But the beast's still twitching. He's just harder to see. – A different prison.

On screen: **John**, *younger, making a speech.*

Caption: Press Awards, London.

It's two-thousand-and-two. I get this award for articles I wrote on war crime. It's late. There's been a lot of booze and we're at that time of the night when people are starting to say what they think. – Opposite me is a woman. She's white. Groomed. The wife of someone famous. – She smiles at me. – Often. – It's a smile I can't read. – The talk turns to race. There's a change of heat. It's one I know well. People are feeling their way – I'm the only person of colour. – The table falls silent. Attention's on me – and she's smiling again. – Now, she speaks: 'We were just saying how good it is someone like you has won an award.' – This demands a response: 'Like me?' I ask. Not skipping a beat, she smiles again: 'Your people.' – I catch the eye of my editor – pleading. – Knowing I could be killing my career, I push on: 'Race is not about colour of skin, ma'am, or silky locks. It's a social construct. It fabricates contrast then inflates it to uniform belief. It's an unspoken contract to see others as underlings, as ominous – unworthy. It's a system that keeps the privileged in power and endorses the kind of remark you just made.' – I smile back, take in the shock around me and walk away – but I feel no different to facing skinheads in Balham as a kid.

Pause.

Then, I sense my father's hand on my shoulder.

On screen: photo of fleeing Sowetan children.

March, nineteen-seventy-six. Thousands pour onto the streets of Soweto. The police open fire. Seven hundred people die, sniped at, shot in the back, or facing down their killers. Their crime? Protest – led by children – against the world's most vicious race laws, where they are forced to be taught in the language of the oppressor. A watershed for South Africa and the watching world. Why my dad fled. – A year later the great Steve Biko is murdered and there'll be another two decades of white dictatorship. – Of Apartheid.

Pause.

Like 'Nazi', it's a word ever more misused and reduced. – So, let's be clear: no sex between white and black; no marriage; detention without trial; torture. A carefully constructed form of social and political oppression against people of colour. Put simply: the closest thing to Nazism the world has ever known with racism enshrined in the constitution. A new political faith for the white man. The work of the devil. That – is Apartheid.

Pause.

But. Ask most people what it was where it was why it happened few have a clue. Even some black kids don't want to be burdened by history. By trauma. They may have a point. Sometimes we need to get out of jail.

On screen: a final harrowing image of Soweto.

My dad was in the thick of it. Round him kids took bullets. And it impelled him to fight back harder.

On screen: photo of a weeping black mother at a hearing of the truth and reconciliation commission.

And when Apartheid fell at last, he had no Christian forgiveness. 'John', he said. 'Remember: most men who murdered their black victims with impunity were never brought to book. They cried crocodile tears before righteous panels and got off Scot-free. Forgiveness trumping justice.'

On screen: the image snaps off.

He was a practical man, my father. There's a time to talk he said, and a time to reach for the baseball bat. It's a rule I lived by.

Pause.

Then one day on a train, I met Marius Muller.

Blackout

Scene Two

Spot on **Marius**.

His back is to us. He is a big man.

A sound: the fluttering of tiny wings – it swells and swells . . . until it engulfs us.

Marius *clutches his ears.*

Marius   FOK WEG!

The sound cuts dead.

Marius *turns slowly to us. His accent is heavily Afrikaans.*

It isn't easy. Talking. But I must.

He comes closer.

Zero's been easy. Always. – Jusses. Nothing as off-putting as self-pity, hey? (*He laughs.*)

Pause.

Example of hardship, you say? – Simple, my friends: Kamieskroon. Now – think of a clapped-out British resort, swap the cottages with shacks walled by scrub and hammered by wind then chuck in a few howling dogs you get the picture. Did I say the train? – Sorry. One of the impacts of war's on memory. With me, anyway. I get these hiccups. Gaps. It's not dementia – though fuck knows that'll come – but a short circuit that means chats like this get a piggyback – doubt. – Have I said that already?'

Pause.

Where in fuck were we? – Language, Marius! – I'm in
England now, hey? – Trains. The old steam train that ran
from Cape Town to Kimberley passed by our farm. Kamies
was typical: pure Apartheid long before it was official.
Coloured workers in their pondoks away from the white
farms they worked. And before you get all riled up about the
word 'Coloured' it's what mixed-race people of the Cape call
themselves. – Here's Kamies:

*On screen: Kamieskroon – as he has described it. A bleak,
windswept Karoo Town.*

Then this.

*On screen: two groups standing either side of a railway track: black
workers one side and white families / farmers on the other.*

A sound: approaching steam train.

In seventy-seven that old train made its last journey.
Something died that day. What it was who can say? We all
turned out to pay our respects: the whites and Coloured
workers from the farms. It showed the heart of the place was
beating strong. Though it was the gat of the world, people
were crying. Both sides of the line.

The sound of the steam train reaches a crescendo then cuts dead.

Not me. I cried when I cut my toe in half on some glass as a
laaitie and my pa beat me till I was raw. His cure for pain
was to inflict some more. Only time I cried since was when
that train went past. I cried alone.

Pause.

They say all kids know is what they're born into and even the
worst places on earth seem normal if you grow up there. It
was like that for me. First time I wore anything on my feet
was when I went to the army.

*On screen: Marius as an eighteen-year-old soldier in the nutria
browns of the South African defence force, beaming at camera.*

Too soon. Take it off, please. TAKE IT OFF!

The screen goes blank.

Sorry for that.

Pause.

It's a honour to be here tonight, so I can talk about myself and about war. – And John. The bloke you think you know. Famous. Rich. Blessed with the words of a king. – He's different to the blacks I met back home. – I got to say it, man, say it like it was, is, in my memory, 'cause if I don't tell the truth of what I was, how things were, what's the fucking point? – And the truth is that other than the Coloureds I knew on the farm and the gooks I killed as a operative, I met few blacks till I came here. To your country. In fact, I can say I'd never had a proper chat with anyone black. The farmworkers back then, back home, were different – half them, half us. – Wait. I lie. I met one.

Pause.

After I was klaared out – sorry, 'demobbed' – back in eighty-nine, I was in such kak shape I've no memory of the six months between then and my moment of 'lucidity' – I've grown to love that fucking word. My psychologist, English Norman, used it when I told him that one day I woke up and found myself in the Sinai desert. How I ended up in a piece of Egypt once seized by Israeli forces I'll never know, but I did. Right on the border. – Anyway, I saw this bunch of IDF paras on patrol, and one of them was black. That inky kind of black that's really, really, black. I went up to them and stared. The black one came to me and asked if I was okay. He had this funny accent. Not like the Jews. Like he was from Africa. And he was. A Falasha sprung to Israel because they said they were Jews and their DNA said they weren't tuning kak. He asked me where I was from, and I lied. But he sussed my accent.

Pause.

And he spat in my face. – This black Jew in Egypt spoeging on a white Boer and it was then the slowest penny on earth dropped and I got how much everyone hated the country I loved with all my heart, the country I'd killed for, the country I'd fled because at eighteen I didn't have a fucking clue who I was any more.

Pause.

You know about Angola?

Pause.

You know about the Second World War, right? The kings and queens of England? A bit about Vietnam? The latest hit on Netflix?

On screen: a lantern slide of shocking images covering the Angolan border war, over –

The Angolan war saw the biggest battles in Africa since Tobruk. It drew in the Chinese, Cubans, with secret chats between Brits, Yanks and Russians. It helped kill Apartheid and sparked Mandela's release. Don't worry. I fought in that war and had no fucking clue what I was fighting for or who was involved and the state blocked news about the kak going down there demanding we swore a vow of silence – so why the fuck would you know? There's enough shit going on in the world.

Pause.

But it's all a big fucking domino stack, right? One black klonkie has his legs blown off by a mine in Angola and there's a ripple effect. And we know ripples become rollers that morph to tsunamis and we all know what the fuck happens next. So – knowing shit can be important – to me, anyway. – I've gone away from Kamies now, haven't I?

Pause.

That night, after the last train, I sat out in the veld with my dog, Kippie. I was ten years old. There was this fat moon high up. I could still hear the doef doef doef of the train in my head as it passed. My gut juddered and I started to blub. Then Kippie lifted his head and looked at the sky and howled. And something in me lifted, man. Made me strong again. And that night, with that dog, in that place, I knew who I was. But from the age of eighteen, after Angola, till that day on the train from Scotland – ten years – I'd lost all sense of that.

Pause.

Then I met John Josana.

Blackout.

Scene Three

Sound of a moving train.

On screen: passing landscape.

Caption: United Kingdom, 1997.

John *is seated at a carriage table. He is reading.*

There is a ding-dong heralding an announcement.

Announcement (*tannoy*)   This is the King's Cross service. Our next stop is Waverley. We apologise for the lack of available seating.

Marius *appears, carrying a rucksack, looks for a vacant seat, sees* **John**, *hesitates, then walks over cautiously. He hovers.*

John *looks up, doesn't engage, looks back at the book.*

Marius *continues to hover.*

John   No other space, mate, may as well sit.

Marius   Thank you.

Something in **Marius**'s *accent has caught* **John**'s *attention. But he doesn't look up from his book.*

Marius *settles opposite, places the rucksack beside himself and glances out at the landscape, then back at* **John**.

He doesn't take his eyes off him.

John *feels the heat of the stare, looks up and meets* **Marius**'s *gaze.*

They stay that way for an unnervingly long time.

Finally, **Marius** *looks away and out at the passing landscape.*

Marius   Green.

John *looks up from his book.*

Marius   Out there. Green, green, green.

John   UK, mate.

Marius   Ja.

He smiles.

John   Not a chatter.

John *continues to read.*

Marius *continues to stare at him.*

Finally, **John** *looks up.*

John   What?

Marius   Just saw Scotland. First time.

Pause.

Not a chatter.

John *resumes reading.*

Marius *continues to stare.*

Marius   One question.

John *sighs, waits.*

Marius   Are your parents from Africa?

John *laughs.*

Marius   I'm curious about people.

John *holds up the book.*

Marius   Won't bother you again.

John *reads.* **Marius** *stares out at the passing landscape.*

Two things now happen simultaneously: lights dim and there is the magnified buzzing sound of a fly.

Both **John** *and* **Marius** *follow its path for a few seconds . . .*

Then the fly lands in the centre of the carriage table between them.

They stare at it.

John *resumes reading.*

The fly starts to buzz around again.

Again, they follow its path.

This time it lands directly in front of **John***.*

They stare at it.

John *slowly raises his book to squash the fly.*

A beat as he takes aim.

Just as he brings the book down, **Marius***, with lightning reflex, snaps a giant hand round* **John***'s wrist, stopping the action mid-air.*

The two men stay frozen like that for a beat, then –

Marius   It's just a tiny soul, trying to find a path to God.

Marius *releases* **John***'s wrist.*

There is a burst of buzzing from the fly.

On screen: it is now clear that the fly has landed on the train window. It settles.

John *looks round to see if there is another available seat.*

There clearly isn't. He starts to read again.

There is a ding-dong heralding an announcement.

Train Guard (*on tannoy*)   There's no trolley service today but if you require refreshments, a counter service is available, selling snacks, drinks and cakes.

Marius *stands and goes down the aisle, exiting.*

John *stares at* **Marius***'s rucksack, looks around again.*

John (*to God*)   Why this guy?

The magnified buzzing starts up again.

John *follows the path of the fly.*

It lands back on the window.

John   Fuck.

Marius *comes back down the aisle and with a beer. He sits.*

This time **John** *stares.*

Marius *does not meet his gaze, looks out.*

John   I think I know where you're from.

Marius   Okay.

Pause.

John   I'm curious about people.

Marius   People like me or people?

Pause.

What about your book?

John   About you.

Marius   Me?

John   Your country.

Pause.

Big day. Three years ago. Democracy.

Marius   Every day's a big day there.

John   You're a Boer.

Pause.

Marius   I'm Afrikaans.

John   Whatever.

Pause.

Marius   And you?

John   Getting your answer.

Marius   Finally.

John   My father was South African.

Pause.

Marius   Mother?

John   Step too far.

Marius   Tell me whatever you want, my friend.

Marius *sticks out a hand.*

John *ignores it.*

John   I'm not especially drawn to Afrikaners.

Marius   You're a big club.

Marius *looks back out of the window.*

John *watches him.*

John   Touching. Your compassion for insects.

Marius *grabs his rucksack, stands, looks around for an empty seat.*

John   One time I'd have punched you for doing what you did.

Marius   Every living thing has a right to life.

John   Is that what they taught you back home? About rights? For insects? How old are you? – Sit. You wanted to talk, so let's fucking talk.

Marius *sits.*

Marius   Wouldn't have been a good idea to hit me.

John   Why's that?

Marius   Twenty-seven.

John   What?

Marius   You asked how old I am. How old are you?

Pause.

We're the same age, I think.

John *looks out of the window.*

Marius   Your pa was South African. Were you born there? Must have come when you were a laaitie. (*Translating.*) 'Boy.' From how you speak. You won't talk about your ma but you say you want to talk – and tell me I'm lucky you didn't hit me.

John   Why's it a good idea?

Marius   What?

John   Not to hit you?

Marius   Ten years of therapy taught me two things – one: you can help even the most traumatised mind.

Pause.

Two: soldiers who've seen combat never lose their kill reflex.

John   Is that what you'd have done? Kill me?

Marius *is still, not taking his eyes off* **John**.

John *bursts out laughing, then suddenly hits the carriage table with force.*

Marius *remains still.*

Marius   I like you. But it's better I sit somewhere else.

John *does not take his eyes off* **Marius***.*

John   Uh-uh. You need to stay.

Pause.

We both know why.

Blackout.

Scene Four

On screen: an iconic German landmark.

Caption: Alexanderplatz, Berlin.

John *in a spot.*

John   My first language was German. Some black exiles found themselves in Eastern Europe with no hope of returning home. While intellectuals like my father were offered refuge, they were also groomed as good communists. And this was the DDR in the mid-seventies. A place where all Nazis had magically vanished. And where some had found roles within the new regime where their talents were appreciated. My father was pragmatic. He said we needed to take help from wherever we could get it. The choices were thin. The West wasn't falling over itself to accommodate people like my father in nineteen-seventy-six. Which is how we landed up in East Berlin.

On screen: a bleak border crossing.

Caption: Checkpoint Charlie, Berlin, 1976.

The story of my father's first border crossing into the DDR was legend among his comrades. I was one year old at the time. But it's been retold so often, I feel like I was a witness. CIA agents recorded all comings and goings. Somewhere, there is a fading polaroid of me as a baby crossing into the East on the back of my father.

A beret and coat are flung at **John** *from the wings.*

A series of camera flashes.

John *puts the clothes on.*

John, *as his father, goes up to an imaginary East German border guard.*

DDR Border Guard (*voice only*)   You are being called, 'George Joshana' – ja?

John (*as his father*)   'Josana' – the 's' is spoken like a 'z'.

DDR Border Guard (*voice only*)   Ich weiß nicht, was dieser schwarze Mann sagt.

On screen: 'I don't know what this black man is saying.'

Pause.

Count to four.

John (*as his father*)   Sorry?

DDR Border Guard (*voice only*)   I am saying, count to four.

John   Why?

DDR Border Guard (*voice only*)   Count to four!

John   Is this some sort of numeracy test?

DDR Border Guard (*voice only*)   COUNT TO FOUR!

John   Alright. One – two – three –

DDR Border Guard (*voice only*)   Nein nein nein, you must go to counter four!

John, *as his father, walks on and as he does, flings the beret and coat back into the wings, then turns to us.*

John   Two things stick with me: the smell of diesel and the thrum of Trabants. Dad never felt easy in the DDR. All that bound him to the place was a safe haven. – It may have been politically safe, but we were few, us blacks. And a kind of curiosity. To be tolerated. Inspected. Boxed. In a place that once gloried in racial supremacy, where they shovelled Jews into gas ovens. And yet, thirty-one years later, while it was another dictatorship, he wasn't being shot at. Or arrested. Or subject to a group areas act. Or living in a fucking shack. So, for him, it was about survival. For himself, and his baby boy. But the gulf was to prove so great it took every ounce of strength for him to stay sane. Towards the end of our stay my father kept repeating words spoken by Martin Luther King: 'Never forget that everything Hitler did in Germany was legal.' – Then, when I was five, a tri-lingual stateless black kid, we left for London.

Pause.

Why mention East Germany? That day on the train with the Boer, I found that we had a few unlikely things in common.

Blackout.

Scene Five

On screen: a black and white photo of a young man, looking remarkably like **Marius***, dressed in SS uniform, with a swastika armband, smiling at camera.*

Marius   Pa.

Pause.

It's nineteen-thirty-six. He's a top gymnast, goes to Berlin for the Olympics. Falls in love with the place and what's driving it and we all know what that was. After all the sport's over, he stays, learns German, joins the SS and applies for citizenship. Boom. – The Nazis offer glory if he goes on a covert mission with a man called Robey Leibrandt: to be dropped by a German sub off the coast of Namibia they'll enter South Africa and find a way to kill this man:

On screen: South African Prime Minister Jan Smuts, 1942.

Jan Smuts. The head of state, an Afrikaner who loved Britain so much he was against the Nazis. Pa finds himself in Namibia six months later and not being a man of much genius bungles his mission at the get-go and is arrested at the border. Spends the war in jail with a few of the country's next prime-ministers and leaves in disgrace, skulking back to Kamies as the Nazi lover who fucked it all up. If he'd got over the border like Leibrandt he'd have been a folk-hero, but he was hated by both sides as a fascist clown. And we could've been twins me and him. To look at. And his self-hatred found a perfect escape.

Marius *draws his belt from his trousers and proceeds to beat his invisible childhood self, becoming his father, whose Afrikaans is translated on screen.*

(As his father.) JY PATETIESE KLEIN KAK, JY SAL SLIM WORD AS DIT DIE LAASTE DING WAT EK DOEN – OM 'N PAAR BREIN IN JOU TE KLOP!

On screen: 'You pathetic little shit, you will become smart if it's the last thing I do to beat some brains into you.'

Didn't work, did it?

Pause.

I was the toughest, strongest, quickest, most unhappy kid in Kamieskroon till the day I joined the army. And then? I entered heaven. It seemed all my fine qualities were a gift to the men who took me under their wing.

Pause.

Now you can show it.

On screen: earlier shot of **Marius** *in military uniform.*

Blackout.

Scene Six

Sounds of a train.

On screen: passing British landscape.

John *is sitting on his own.*

Marius *appears with two bottles of beer, sits.*

He places one in front of **John**.

John *stares at it.*

Marius   You don't drink?

Pause.

You won't drink with me. – But you want to talk? – You say.

Pause.

Tell me about your book.

John *holds the book up and shows* **Marius** *the cover.*

John   Robben Island. Where men now leading your country were once called terrorists. Where the new state president and former public enemy, Mr Mandela, was held for two decades. Where intellectuals were imprisoned by imbeciles. Where they buried people upright, heads exposed to the sun, then pissed on them for sport.

Pause.

Marius   You're angry.

John *laughs.*

But the laugh quickly vanishes.

Damn fucking right.

Marius   You should be.

He takes a long slug of beer.

Must've been just one school of torture back home 'cause all styles seem the fucking same. My pa had this rack of canes. Each of them had a name. To fit the crimes of his son. Tarzan, Delilah, Cheeky and Piet. Piet was thin and long and made me bleed. He tied my ankles to the feet of a chair and made me face the wrong way round with my arms flopped over the back legs. Took a long run up like a bowler. The kids in our street always knew when I was being hit because of his yelling. They'd line up outside the shed. Waiting. The aim was not to cry. Not to give them that pleasure. Whatever pain I was in. Shu. I always failed. The day I found him hanging from the roof with his rack of canes tongue all blue and sticking out was the best day of my life. And that day, I smiled.

John *stares at him, unmoved.*

Marius   But what happened to me can't compete with what's going in in that book of yours now, can it, hey? – 'Diejenigen, die Schmerz und Lächeln ertragen können, werden triumphieren' as pa said.

John (*translating*)   Those that can take pain and smile will triumph.

Marius *is taken aback.*

John   Interesting quote. Triumphed, did he? Like you?

John *holds up the book again.*

What happened, matters. What happened to people. My people. Black people. Everywhere. The past. All of us. All – of – us. We own it. Together. Forever. And we all need to take a long hard look at it. Work out what's real and what isn't. Tear down the statues. Chuck out the lies. The stories twisted to make us sleep at night. Like you were taught at school. Replace them with the missing bits. With the truth. And find a link between the horror that went before us and what we still face. – That's what's coming. A nightmare for people like you. A real fucking nightmare.

John *tosses the book across to* **Marius**.

Marius *looks down at the book, then back up at* **John**.

Marius   How come you speak German?

Pause.

John   Do you hear me?

Pause.

I lived there till I was five.

Marius   He lived there too.

John   Who?

Marius   My father. – Nineteen-thirty-six to nineteen-forty-two. He was fifty when I was born.

John   Loved the Nazis, did he?

Marius *laughs.*

Marius   He *was* a Nazi.

John   Like some of your state presidents.

Pause.

Marius   When were you there?

John *looks out at the passing landscape.*

John   Seventy-six to eighty-one.

Marius   Where?

John   The East.

John *reaches for the bottle of beer and drinks, hesitates, then downs the whole bottle.*

Marius   I'm allowed a bottle a week. But today is special.

Pause.

Is your father alive?

Pause.

You said, let's talk.

John   We will.

Pause.

He died three years ago.

Marius   I'm sorry.

John   Why?

Pause.

Marius   I think you worshipped him.

John *doesn't take his eyes off* **Marius**.

Blackout.

Scene Seven

On screen: **John**'s *father in a South African township.*

Capton: George Josana, Soweto, 1976.

Spot on **John**.

John   Last shot of my father before he fled. He's forty. A week after the uprising my mother left him and went back to the Transkei. Ran back home. There was twenty years between them. A tiny baby and activism were too much for her. She left without me. Before I was weaned. She warned him she couldn't cope – but I think her choice to run took him by surprise.

Pause.

As if to prove her point the Soweto massacre meant that the security police were also gunning for people like my father. There was no time to get me to her – and he didn't know if she'd want me if he did. Escape meant dragging a howling infant across African borders and risky checkpoints. Never once did he complain about her but as I grew older and my questioning grew, all he'd say was that he may have misjudged things but no point in blaming her.

Pause.

For me, it was different.

Pause.

The move to London when I was five offered some relief, but a new set of . . . what do we call it? Challenges? I think that's the weasel word these days. The UK in eighty-one for a foreign black kid whose first language was German demanded focus.

On screen: images of the Yorkshire Ripper, Enoch Powell, Bobby Sands in the Maze Prison, John Lennon's murder, IRA bombing of Chelsea Barracks.

The exile community was small, and my time was split between a regime in waiting made up of intellectuals and radicals talking tactics by night, and tricky integration into school by day. My father was often away and wept when he returned at the change in me, to which he was unable to 'bear witness,' as he said. For me, as a boy, it was as if God had appeared.

Pause.

One question stuck, a question that always seemed to spark the same response, offered with a sage-like patience, and which, as I grew older, gnawed at me. 'Will you ever try to find her? Will you ever, Papa?' A hand shoots to my shoulder, I'm peered at over the top of his specs, and in that basso-profundo he replies: 'Your mama is fearful of what I do, fear is her master, and she knows where we are. If she wants to find us, she will.'

Pause.

When he died, I got this letter. Twenty years after we'd left. She begged my forgiveness, said she was haunted and hurting. If I was ever home, I must make contact. – All about her.

Pause.

Like she did when she fled, I exercised a choice. Not to respond.

Pause.

Not provide – absolution.

Pause.

Then, two years later, on that train, with the Boer, I was saddled with another religious dilemma – one that would become linked to her and that finally led to a long invasion of my family and my past.

Blackout.

Scene Eight

Marius *in a spot.*

On screen: soldiers marching across a bleak parade ground; corrugated barracks in the background.

Caption: Lenz Military Camp, South Africa 1988.

Marius *is still, facing us, then:*

Marius   Dui! Afdeling – AANDAG!

Marius *snaps to attention.*

Pause.

Easy. All that was asked of me I'd done since I could walk: shoot, fight, keep clothes, kit, sharp, obey orders, no questions asked. The marching was a piece of cake. The route runs. The routine. They were fucking obsessed with marching. With precision. Cleanliness. Ritual put us in three: Roofies – battered recruits, blougatte – 'blue-arses' the half broken-in, and oumanne – conscripts near the end of their time, top of the pile. A blessing. The longer you were there the more you were ignored. Grading was all. It gave order. Stability. It boosted and belittled, vital to the smooth-running of an army. I fitted in well. I was respected. – Feared. My pa had trained me to perfection for my new calling. And for what I was to become.

Pause.

Op die plek – RUS!

He stands at ease.

Pause.

On my second weekend pass, I found him dangling from the beams in his shed. Just months after I left. No one to torture any more. Ma was long dead. A death he never explained. One day she was there then she was gone. As a three-year-old such things are easy to accept.

John (*from the darkness*)   Not curious, then? It's your mother.

Sounds of the train.

Lights up on the two men, facing each other across the carriage table.

There are now at least a dozen empty beer bottles between them.

On screen: the passing landscape is urban.

Marius   Whatever family she had never tried to find me. So, who fucking cares? My psychologist, English Norman, said it would be good for 'healing,' but you can only heal where there's a fucking wound, am I right? And there's none with her. With Ma. I never really knew her.

Pause.

And yours?

Pause.

'A step too far,' hey? Even after six hours and ten beers.

John   You talk of him a lot.

Marius   Who?

John   Norman.

Marius   He found me in the Sinai. This little Englishman hitched to this Israeli chick. They were on holiday. He saw that black Jew gobbing on me, and we talked. My granny left me money in her will. I spent it all on him. From that day to now.

John   Helped you then, has he? You're a perfectly balanced immigrant-cum-Apartheid-lover who sleeps well at night.

Marius *is still.*

Marius   Excuse me.

Marius *stands and exits.* **John** *downs the last beer.*

Train Guard (*on tannoy*)   Our next stop is King's Cross, King's Cross next stop.

On screen: rain starts to lash the window.

John *begins to tidy away his things from the carriage table.*

Marius *reappears and watches* **John** *from a distance.*

John *becomes aware of him and looks up.*

Marius *returns to his seat.*

Marius   You never get nightmares?

John   What?

Marius   Nightmares. Seem so certain of it all.

John   That right?

Pause.

John   What am I certain about?

Marius   Me.

Pause.

John   Nightmares?

Pause.

Marius   Yes.

John   Alright, then. How about the Congo. *The Nun's Story.*

Marius   The what?

John   I saw this film called *The Nun's Story* when I was a kid. Before I knew better. All about the dilemma of some white woman sent to Africa where she has a revelation about faith. In it, said nun, Audrey Hepburn, is lured into this nutter's cell in a mental asylum and attacked by an inmate who thinks she's the archangel Gabriel and beats herself with whips. And for the next year I couldn't sleep. Every night the curtains billowed and in crept this bleeding angel come to rip me to bits. I was ten at the time, an artless little bugger and the image of a mad self-harming shrew through some religious delusion freaked the fuck out of me. Does that work for you?

Pause.

But these days, I seldom have nightmares.

Marius   What do you have?

Pause.

Marius *tries to drink another beer. Realises the bottle is empty.*

John   Look at me.

Marius *places the bottle back on the carriage table and looks at* **John***.*

John   I owe you nothing, you understand? You sat across from me on a train and yacked about yourself for hundreds of miles while we drank a few ales. That's it. But there's no deal here, get it? No agreement. No – connection. No surprise your dad loved Hitler. The fucking country you grew up in had racism enshrined in its constitution. And you fought for its supremacist army. The black kids on the streets of Soweto in seventy-six were your age when you pulled on those army boots, denied the rights you took for granted, yet they knew. They knew what was what.

Marius   Why'd you tell me that story?

John   You asked if I had nightmares.

Marius   I think you don't talk about your ma because you can't talk about her, am I right? None of my business of course.

John *laughs.*

Marius   Just your pa you like to mention. The ANC hero. You've been driving that home for hours. Certain it's going to get to me. Certain you know who I am.

John   Who are you?

The fly starts to buzz around again.

They follow its path. **Marius** *sits back in his seat.*

Marius   Maybe it's time.

John   Time?

Marius   For me to talk.

John   What the fuck have we been doing for the past five hours?

Marius   I think you know the answer.

Marius *looks out of the window. He takes in a deep breath, taps his temples with the index finger of each hand repeatedly, as if he is readying himself for something for which he has long prepared.*

Finally, he turns to **John**.

Marius   My basic training was three months. Within a fortnight I was chosen for Parabats, this elite fighting force. Soldiers flung from planes onto enemy ground to kill. The Angolan war was in full swing and ten weeks later I was the youngest conscript ever seconded to the country's most brutal unit: the Special Forces.

He looks back at **John.**

Marius   At eighteen I was shoulder to shoulder with trained killers who stopped at nothing for Apartheid. Deep into enemy terrain by night. Laying low for days. Then you know what.

The fly starts to buzz again.

This time **John** *swats it dead on the carriage table.*

Marius *stares at the result.*

John   Talk.

Marius   Six months into my service I'd seen a lot of death. A few SWAPO operatives had copped it in combat. And that was just me.

Pause.

By the end I was 'bosbefok'. (*Translating.*) 'Bushfucked.' Or as English Norman calls it: 'War trauma in action.'

Pause.

Now, if you want to know more and I think you do from the way you've been pushing things you'll have to go back to those feelings you had as a laaitie watching that film about the nun. – But they may never go away.

Pause.

You ready?

Pause.

You think you know all about the country of your father because you read some books? Because him and his pals told you things? I can tell you some first-hand kak if you've got the guts.

John *doesn't take his eyes off* **Marius**.

The screen slowly fades to black and all sound cuts dead but for their voices.

Marius On a recce our unit caught what we called a 'gook' – a black terrorist – a 'freedom fighter' you'd call it – trying to enter my country. He had a wound so deep you could see the bones of his neck. The wound seemed fatal. I was ordered to guard him for the night. We sat out in the open. He was propped up against a tree.

Pause.

He begged me to kill him . . . hour after hour . . . his retching and writhing were driving me insane. I didn't know how to help him or if I'd be court-martialled if I did. Help him end it, that is. Before his next interrogation. Seven hours went by. His cries were like the whining of dying fox. I could see the top of his spine. I started to hallucinate.

Pause.

Finally, I slid my knife into the wound to sever it quick. End it. End the night. I had to saw the thing. Took me five minutes.

Pause.

When his head came off there was this hissing sound. Like his soul was leaving his body.

The sound again: the fluttering of wings.

I thought I saw something flying into the night sky. It seemed like a kind of a moth. I'll never know what it was but since that day I wake every night to the sound of tiny wings fluttering over my head.

John *stares at him.*

Then he stands. He is shaking with rage.

The sound of the fluttering wings swells and swells . . . until it engulfs us.

John *draws back his fist.*

The sound cuts dead.

On screen: the train enters King's Cross.

People get off and pass the window.

John *and* **Marius** *are still, taking each other in.*

Finally, **John** *lowers his fist.*

Marius   Thank you.

Pause.

John   Thank you? – Thank you? – For what? For – WHAT? Took you the whole journey to crank up to that lovely little story, did it? Six hours. Ten beers? What were you doing? – Finding the guts? Having fun? – Jerking off? – Is that the tough old tale you told the Truth Commission? A sad story all about you? About your suffering? Your mighty ordeal? About some stupid bloody MOTH? After you chopped off the head of your dying black captive? And did they weep big fucking tears AT YOUR SEARING FUCKING HONESTY?

Pause.

Marius   I am my own judge.

Sound: the wings start to flutter.

John *leans in close.*

John   Then ask yourself this: why you chose to behead him.

The fluttering grows louder.

Slowly.

And louder.

Marius   You've never been in battle.

John   Save me the war trauma.

Marius   We were a unit.

John   The 'I was just a foot soldier'.

Marius   I was fucked in the head, man.

The fluttering reaches a climax then cuts dead.

John   You made a choice.

Marius   Fucked.

John   You chose to behead him.

Marius   I was born in it. I grew up in it. It's all I fucking knew.

John   Your father would have been proud of you.

Pause.

You sick lunatic.

John *gathers up his things and steps into the aisle and walks away down the aisle.*

Marius   I don't know your name.

John *has gone.*

Blackout.

Act Two

Scene One

John *in a spot.*

John My father's gift was certainty. He was of an age driven by big ideas. An age filled with great men and great women, unafraid when it came to calling out cant in their enemies, their comrades and themselves. The unsung heroes of the struggle whose names are all but forgotten: Biko, Sobukwe, Sisulu, Ramphele.

Pause.

By the time change came in ninety-four, I was a grown man. A nineteen-year-old Cambridge student. Rooted in Britain. With my eyes on the world and the streets of London. While South Africa was my father's obsession, other things were happening. Momentous things. The Kremlin Accords; genocide in Rwanda; civil war in Yemen; the invasion of Chechnya.

On screen: Mandela's inauguration as president of South Africa.

My dad's plan was to return home with me so we could fling ourselves into building what he called 'the world's greatest democracy'.

Pause.

The night before we left, he clutched his chest, grinned at me and dropped down dead.

On screen: a mass funeral and wake in London.

Sound: soft humming of Nkosi S'kelele.

Six hundred people came to his cremation. I'd no idea how widely he was admired till that day. I was crushed.

The humming cuts dead.

But as time passed, I was forced to admit I was also relieved. The thought of returning to a country I'd fled with him as a baby, that had caused him so much pain, was . . . not easy. The letter from my mother hinting at absolution was the seal. But if we are dealing in absolute truth tonight – there was the fact that my career as a journalist was taking off.

Pause.

And the reason was simple: Marius Muller.

Blackout.

Scene Two

Marius *in a spot.*

Marius   After the Middle East I buggered back home. Norman wrote to me each week. He was obsessed. Even after my cash ran out.

Pause.

There was fuck all for me in Kamies. The house was worthless. I've never sold it to this day. I left after a week. And that was thirty years ago. Who knows what state it's in now. It's my gift. To him. To Pa. There's no hate. There's nothing. Just a space where the past sits and never moves. That needs no check-up, whatever the fuck Norman says. I talk about Angola but never him. My Pa. He dangles in my memory with his canes.

He hits himself, hard – then breathes in to steady himself.

I'm lying.

Pause.

I'm trying to impress you. The need to seem strong makes us all liars. I think about pa all the time.

On screen: **Marius** *in uniform, beside his father.*

I came home twice when I was in the army. First time, I got a message from someone in Kamies to say Pa was acting odd. He was already odd. So, it meant he must be off the fucking rails. I used my first weekend pass to go see him. Maybe the sight of me in uniform would mean something. But all he could talk about was his time in Berlin. How nothing matched it. How no nation on earth would ever know the joy the Germans felt in the years before the war.

Marius's *body shape seems to change.*

(*As his father.*) Look at me when I talk to you. There was a time when I held destiny in these hands. If I'd got to that English gat-kruiper Jannie Smuts the Cape would've fallen to us and with it a vital sea-route. Tell that to your fat CO, your sergeants, who think controlling a few million blacks is some big fucking deal. We were half an inch from ruling the fucking world. Now salute me. Salute me before I beat you raw like I did in the shed. HET JY MY SO FOKKIN FYN?

On screen: 'Do you fucking understand me?' Then his father's image returns.

Pause.

He was with me all the time in Angola. Watching. Judging. (*Staring at the image of his father.*) Please remove it now.

The screen goes blank.

Marius *turns away from us.*

After a few moments, he turns back.

Marius *removes a newspaper cutting from his pocket.*

Pause.

From the *Guardian* in ninety-eight, ten months after I met John. I'll cut to the chase.

Marius *sucks in a deep breath.*

(*Reading from article.*) 'The sadism he'd endured as a boy from his fascist father was reborn in the bush, where his victims knew no mercy. Yet in this hulking Afrikaner, there was a need to talk.'

Spot on **John**.

Marius *watches* **John** *as he reads.*

John (*reading from article*)   'Whatever his analyst offered in those long years seemed to have no impact on his torment. The root of that torment was harder to discern in our brief time together.'

Marius (*to us*)   He puts words together nice, am I right? (**Marius** *reads from article*.) 'His story repelled and fascinated. That slow beheading and fantasy moth drifting into the night sky haunted him.'

Marius *catches his breath, steadies himself.*

John (reading)   'Yet, it seemed vital to recount the event in all its pornographic detail and want of humanity. In his view, he was doing that captive a favour. I came to realise that the need to offload the horror eclipsed any sense of remorse, like a child who purges a nightmare by sharing it with a parent. Or a man riddled with poison who is comforted by passing it on to others – he needed to draw me into his hell.'

Marius (*to us*)   I'm trying – I am trying – to find me – in all of this.

John (*reading*)   'For those six hours I had been the father he had never had. The priest. Or maybe, the sitting duck. But another question lingered: why, in that long train to London, he had chosen me. – Was it white guilt? Moral conscience? Or was it something he didn't get himself, something simpler – that he was asking me, as a black man, to feel sorry for him. And to offer a way out of his torment. Whatever was driving him, he failed to grasp a simple fact: that every white person living under the regime that led to his horrific crime benefited from white supremacy whether they liked it or not – and that I was the last person on earth he should approach for forgiveness.'

The spot on **John** *snaps off.*

Marius (*to us*)   I try to think what Norman might make of this. – Nothing comes. But three words keep humming in my kop. 'Flukse fokkin' bliksem.' The meaning may be too tough for you.

On screen: 'Smart fucking bastard.'

They're only efficient, here, hey?

Pause.

The first time I knew of his articles on me was last year. A long time after they first came out. Someone had read them all and knew it was me he was writing about. He never used my name. He did me that courtesy. But how many eighteen-year-olds grew up in a dorp in the middle of nowhere with a useless Nazi father whose son fought in Angola? (*He laughs.*) Quite a few, maybe. Though to anyone who knew me and knew my pa it would've been easy to see who the fuck it was. And identify me. And there was one person who knew him well. Though I hadn't seen them since I was a kid. Someone I thought was dead.

Pause.

My Ma.

Blackout.

Scene Three

Spot on **John**.

John   I didn't give the man another thought after that day on the train. I'd met someone in Scotland and we'd fallen in love. My wife, Orla. Within a week I'd moved in with her.

For the first time things seemed effortless. My self-absorption was seen as part of the deal.

Pause.

Then ten months after the train journey.

Blackout.

On screen: a circle of light.

I'm in a tunnel. It's dark but there's a circle of light ahead.

Footsteps on gravel.

Like a Hitchcock movie, my footsteps echo, my shadow tracks me as I move.

A soft fluttering of wings.

Then I hear it. Wings fluttering. Without turning I know what it is. Some great insect is hovering behind me, its wingspan blocks out the light.

The circle of light diminishes to a dot as the fluttering increases in volume.

Then it lands, latching on, and its proboscis shoots into my neck. The life force is sucked out of me and there's nothing I can do.

The fluttering wings cut dead.

Orla shakes me awake. The sheets are wet. I'm laughing now. She asks what I was dreaming about. Then my laughter stops. Because I recall a detail from the dream. Powder falling on me in the attack. From the wings of a giant moth.

Lights up on **John**.

I replayed the meeting on the train. Was I a target? Were those hours of chat grooming me for a confession? How many people had he told? Whatever the truth, he'd passed the horror on to me. I told Orla what had happened. And she pushed me to write about it. And attend to the anger I felt. It wasn't hard. Overall, that's a useful emotion when it comes to writing. Specially for me.

Pause.

When the third piece was published, a letter came. The writer clearly didn't know of the articles or the instant acclaim they'd brought me. (*Reading* **Marius**'s *letter.*) 'I'm sorry I told you that story. I still don't know why I did.'

Spot on **Marius**.

Marius   But I forgive you. Your anger. I understand. What I did must have seemed to someone like you so filled with sin it goes beyond what anyone could understand.

Marius *looks at us, then back at his own letter.*

John   'Someone like you.' – That phrase again. A phrase I was to hear years later from a white woman at a press award.

Marius (*reading*)   'But after we met something happened. Though I spent ten years talking to a psychologist, I can't find the words to describe it. All I can say is, the fluttering of wings almost stopped that day. I now work for a global foundation helping soldiers with PTSD. Most of our work is in Africa. Yours sincerely, Marius.'

The spot on **Marius** *goes off.*

John   *He* – forgives – *me*?

Pause.

It was then I chose to stop. Thinking about him. Digging. Giving his pain oxygen. Pain without so much as a nod to the racist doctrine that led to his monstrous crime. And that made his quest for redemption obscene. Finally, I felt free of the virus, free of him and free of the moth.

Blackout.

Scene Four

On screen: **John**, *older, standing with a white woman and three mixed race children in front of a large home.*

Caption: Hampstead, London.

John *is centre stage typing on a laptop.*

Marius *appears.*

He watches **John**.

John *spins round and sees* **Marius**.

John   Fuck!

Marius   Your wife let me in.

Pause.

It's me.

John   I can see that.

Pause.

'Let you in'?

Marius   Knew me. Straight off.

Pause.

John   How'd you find me.

Marius   Hard work.

John's *phone rings on intercom.*

John   Hello?

Pause.

No, it's fine.

He hangs up.

Marius   Is she worried?

John   Should she be?

Pause.

Marius   Well done on your success. Your fame. Those talks you do. The people you grill. The words you pull together. Quite something. Your 'Confessional'. Nothing gets past you, hey?

Marius *gazes out of a window.*

Green, green, green.

Pause.

You've got a beautiful home.

Pause.

John   How's your . . . work? – The soldiers?

Pause.

Marius   Why did you stop?

John   Stop?

Pause.

Writing about you?

Marius   You write nice. Like in a book.

Pause.

My work with the vets stopped.

Pause.

I'm a janitor now. In a college.

John   Why did *you* stop?

Marius   Got in too deep.

John   Isn't that the point?

Marius   People think they know what it's like. Uh-uh. Not even the most gruesome movie comes close. Stuff those guys talked about. Stuff harder than what I told you. Worse than the nun. Like you wouldn't believe. – Babies.

John   Stop.

Marius   Ja. – That's it, my friend. War's not pretty.

Pause.

John   Why are you here?

Pause.

Marius   You made me famous.

John   If we can call it that.

Pause.

Spit it out. You want an apology?

Marius   For what? You saw what you had to see.

John   And what did I see?

Marius   Someone who couldn't grasp what they'd really done.

John   What did you really do?

Marius   Chop off the head of a dying man when I could have made . . . other choices.

John   And what were those?

Marius   You're on good form.

Pause.

You once came at me about how I did it. How I killed him. – Was that a choice? – But let's not get back into that.

John   No.

Marius   Maybe I could have shot him. I could also have shot my CO. Or I could have gone AWOL. But then he'd have died slowly. That gook. Each of those would have meant court martial. And a long fucking time in jail.

Pause.

There was another choice.

John   Oh, yes?

Marius   I could have shot myself.

The phone intercom rings.

John *answers.*

John   Mum's right, you can't come up for a while. I know I promised. But I have a guest.

He hangs up.

We need to draw this to a close.

Marius   I went home for a bit, you know. I couldn't find a job. I was one of those bearded white guys standing in the road, a sign round the neck. 'Marius Muller. Twenty-six. No work. Hungry.' I stayed in a squatter camp for poor whites. When we begged, the shame was so big we stood like statues. In the sun. Rain. People were shocked to see whites begging.

John   Which people?

Marius *nods and smiles.*

Marius   You were right. About me. About many things. You're a smart man. But there's one thing you were wrong about.

John   Oh, yes?

Marius   The story. You. And that's why I need to be here. To set the record straight.

John   The record?

Marius   You were the first person I ever told. The only person. Now, everyone knows. But you never named me.

John   Would you like to have been named?

Marius   I didn't choose you that day on the train. Someone else did.

John   And who would that be?

Pause.

Marius   I *was* recognised, you know. From those things you wrote.

John   Oh, yes?

Marius   It was easy for her.

John   Her?

Marius   My ma.

John   You said she was dead.

Marius   She was. According to Pa.

On screen: **Marius**'s *father, beside him, a young woman in a cotton dress.*

He could've been her pa. She was a orphan at sixteen. He was fifty, a pal of her parents. His first shame was ballsing up that mission for the Nazis. The second was marrying Ma after he got her pregnant. – She was a kid with a kid. – You can add that to our two stories. The criss-cross.

Pause.

We're both still curious, am I right? And you like a good story. Helps with your work. So, you can add runaway mommies to the things that show we have a connection.

John   Do we?

Marius   You wrote all those things about me, my boet, and if we hadn't met that day on the train I wonder if you'd be sitting in this kief home with a pretty wife and happy kids tapping away on a Mac. My nightmare was your gift, am I right? You took me apart. Bit by bit. But it was just scraps of

Marius. Pulled together by a writer in a way that worked for him. And made the good people of Britain clap.

John   And how would it have worked for you?

Marius   NOW PLEASE, MY FRIEND I'M JUST ASKING YOU TO LISTEN!

Pause.

John   Let me see if I've got it right: you hunted me down and burst in after twenty years to tell me you chose me to unburden yourself of your atrocity and inform me of more revelations you want me to put into print for the world to read even though I don't understand you and yet I should be grateful to you for having a career.

Marius   You should have been a lawyer.

John   HAMBA LA!

The phone rings.

John *answers.*

John   Everything's fine. – I'm sure.

John *hangs up.*

You need to leave my home.

Marius   I need to thank you for something.

John *takes a step towards* **Marius**.

Marius   You joined me to my ma again. She didn't die. She fell for a man. A Scots man who came to Kamies to buy land for a farm only to see it was the kakkest place on earth. But he met Ma. And she ran off with him. She wrote to pa saying she wanted to come get me. He met her with a sjambok and said if she ever came back he'd kill us all. She lives in Scotland. I spent time there and never knew. Till I met you.

John *is unreadable.*

Marius *stands and hands* **John** *a photo.*

On screen: **Marius**, *standing beside an African woman of about seventy, against a rural Transkei setting.*

Marius   Payback.

Pause.

She said you wouldn't know who she was. She lives in Coffee Bay. At the mouth of the Nenga. The town looks out over a mile of beach.

John *moves closer to* **Marius**.

Marius   Are you going to hit me? Like you nearly did on the train.

Pause.

A week before I left SA for good, I walked into a shop and bought this old Harley. Drove to Transkei. Went into a cop station and asked if they'd help find a lady called Josana married to a man who ran after Soweto. This old guy on a bench piped up: 'She lives in Coffee Bay. I know her.' It was like in a movie. Where things come right when you least expect. She's a sweet lady. Reads all you write. Proud of you like you wouldn't believe. But I was glad she didn't know I was the man in those pieces of yours. Here's her note to you.

Marius *places a note carefully on* **John**'s *desk*.

Marius   She doesn't expect you to respond to her. It's the second one to you, am I right? Said if you don't, she won't bother you again.

Pause.

I found your mother.

John   You're a fucking madman.

Marius   There's a reason we met.

John   My mother? Really? – My mother?

Pause.

I don't need to tell you the damage you've done by doing what you did. – But I think you know that. You're a lot sharper than you pretend to be. Get pleasure from this, do you? This your petty revenge? Some self-serving act to get my attention? – Think you're doing me a favour hunting down a woman I never knew? And never knew because of the fascist regime you fought for? Killed for? That made me and my father stateless? Is this your atonement, then? For your crimes in the bush. Your atrocity? Invading my home and my life? Hunting down a woman who left before I was weaned and who never tried to find me? Till she was old? Till *you* appeared? A killer with a scheme? An executioner? With another fucking note begging forgiveness? – MY MOTHER?

Pause.

All you've done is fuck with my past. Place me under obligation. To someone I'll never see. Who I've no desire to see. Do you understand? You're doing what you did in the bush. A self-serving act of mercy on a man you don't know, making more pain.

Marius   I know you.

John   Yet you don't know yourself. You believe in the world you've spun, Mr. Muller. They say even the devil tells the truth. But it's your fucking truth.

Pause.

We will never meet again. Never have contact. After today you cease in my life.

Marius *looks at the floor, turns his back to* **John**.

He appears to be removing something from his jacket.

Marius *turns back, holding a pistol.*

Marius   Pa brought it back from Berlin. SS issue. He sneaked it in to kill Smuts. Buried it in Namibia and after he

was released dug it up. I'm sorry if I've made bad choices.
You're a great writer. But you don't really know who I am.

Marius *places the barrel in his mouth.*

John   FUCK!

The intercom phone rings and continues to ring.

Listen – to – me. There are three kids downstairs. The
youngest is four. They'll hear the shot. And even if they don't
rush up, they'll know someone's brains were plastered all
over the wall because of the fallout that will come. – The
police – The press. All that fucking trauma. Is that what you
want? – To bring back the moth? Make another fucking
nightmare.

Blackout.

Scene Five

Spot on **John**.

John   He didn't blow his brains out. – I kept thinking of a
story I'd read. This youth trapped on top of a burning bus.
He kicked out a window. Below was a man. The man told
him to jump. Said he'd somehow break the fall. The youth
jumped and landed on the man's back. Like a miracle
neither was hurt. And the story made the press. The guts of
the man on the ground. And his life took off. – I was that
man. But the bloke on my back never got off. Never stopped
talking.

Pause.

After the near suicide in my living room, Marius Muller
went silent.

Blackout.

Sound of an incoming Skype.

The sound of the Skype gets louder and louder, then cuts dead.

Scene Six

Spot on **John**.

John　Ithemba.

Pause.

'I see you have no idea what it means,' she says. – 'It was your nickname as a baby. 'Hope.' – She waits. 'Do you recognise me? Did he show you the photo?' she asks.

Pause.

I'm at my desk. There's an incoming Skype, I can't identify. I'm careful about contact details. And I never answer calls I don't recognise. But there's this chill in my neck. – And this time I answer.

Pause.

'You're shocked,' she says. 'What did I expect?'

On screen: **Joy Josana**, *smiling, in front of her modest Transkei home.*

John　And there she is. The woman who last held me as a howling infant in Soweto fifty years ago. – 'Say something,' she says. 'Anything, even if it's bugger off.'

The image of **Joy** *fades.*

John　I can't speak. – I see myself in her. She looks frail. There's a silence. And all I manage is, 'How did you get my number?' She smiles: 'Your friend, the Afrikaner. He got it from your wife.'

Pause.

My wife and the Afrikaner. Swapping numbers in the moments before he spoke to me on the day he nearly killed himself in my home. And she gave him double access. – Orla. Always on the cracks.

Pause.

As a boy, as a son, I've played this moment out a thousand times. But I chose to stop thinking about her. As if reading my thoughts, she says: 'None of us lives forever, John.'

Pause.

'Marius Muller is not my friend,' I say. She doesn't understand. But it's clear to me: he wouldn't have identified himself as the man in those early pieces I wrote. He would have needed to present himself as my friend. – This killer. This beheader of dying men. – Which it would be wise not to tell her.

Pause.

'Your children. Tell me about your children,' she says.' A minute ago, I was writing a piece about Black Panther Bobby Seale and now I'm face to face with a sixty-nine-year-old woman I haven't seen since I was ripped from her bosom.

Pause.

'Why,' I reply. She shakes her head. 'I see him in you. Your papa. The need to be strong at all costs. Don't be strong, John. Just . . . talk to me.' But as I take her in, images offer themselves: my dad, head in hands, choking on a sob, in some Berlin tenement when I was a boy; the thud of Doc Martens on my ribs as I walk the gauntlet home in Balham as a youth; the months waiting for Dad to return from some far-flung state till I was a grown man.

Pause.

'I'm sorry,' I say to her. 'I've no memory of you. At eight months old memories aren't made. I've no idea who you are. Almost half a century has passed. There's nothing. So, this is not emotional for me.'

Pause.

'For me it is,' she says. 'The most emotional thing I've ever done.' – 'I understand,' I say. 'But I gave no permission for it to take place.' She shakes her head. 'To be angry your whole life, John? What did he tell you? – Your papa?' Orla calls on the intercom. She knew this was planned. And before I can pick up, my mother says, 'She's a wonderful woman. Don't be angry with her.' I let the call ring off. Finally, she is ready to say whatever she's planned: 'I never went with another man. Your father and I were married till the end. But half a century is more than a lifetime. More than anyone could forgive.'

Pause.

I know I must listen. I also know nothing she will say can ever address the past.

John *shuts his eyes.*

On screen: **Joy** *reappears and we hear her voice.*

Joy (*V/O*)   Your father was closing forty when we married. I was nineteen. I worshipped him. As did many. – I ran. Yes, I ran. My only comfort is knowing my boy may never forgive me. Your father . . . (*She is too emotional to continue.*)

John *waits.*

Joy (*V/O*)   Your father saw the future in you. Your birth was everything to him. You offered hope. But in the first months of your life our home was raided ten times. I begged him to come with me to Transkei. He refused. Then the night after Soweto he said we were leaving for Tanzania. The escape would be hard, he said. The choice was simple: let him take you to safety or stay on with the police closing in.

John   You chose not to come.

Joy (*V/O*)   I feared your father. His disapproval. I was a coward. But I knew you'd be safer with him. It took me twenty-five years to write to you. – Then nothing. – You waited and so did I. – Then like some miracle, the Afrikaner appeared.

Joy's *image starts to fade.*

John   'Anything you could say to me I've said every day of my life since you left with your father,' she says. 'Things you can't imagine being said to anyone. In your writing there is great wisdom. Compassion. Reserve some of it for me.'

Pause.

She blows me a kiss then her image is gone.

Blackout.

Scene Seven

On screen: passing landscape.

Sounds of a moving train.

Caption: United Kingdom, the present.

John *is seated at a carriage table, typing on a laptop.*

Marius *appears, sees* **John***, is surprised, walks unsteadily to* **John***.*

John *sees him, is shocked.*

Marius *hovers at the table.*

Marius   I'm not following you. I promise.

Pause.

This is befok.

Pause.

Can I?

John *sighs, indicates he can sit.*

Marius   It's like I can conjure you up.

Pause.

I'm on my way to see my ma and my stepdad. The one who ran away with her.

Pause.

How's your family?

Marius *sits.*

That day. The gun. I . . . I need to say sorry. And I need to tell you something.

Pause.

I get why you say you can have fuck all to do with me. But you know, and please listen, please – we met for a reason. It's why today's happening. Can't you see it? Feel it? You can think I'm nuts. Maybe I am. But I believe in a God, for no other reason than if it's all down to fucking particles and matter we'll never understand, how fucking boring is that?

Pause.

I had to tell my story. I had to tell someone. And then there you were. Like God had sent you to me on that day. And now here you are again.

Pause.

Why?

Pause.

Do you know what 'boet' means? It means 'brother'.

Pause.

Call it fate. Or God. Or destiny. Call it whatever you like. But we will always be connected, my boet. We are locked together, forever. For eternity. And I think you know it.

Pause.

When I killed those men and did what I did in the bush to that dying gook, in the end there was only one person in front of me and that was me. You did more for me in eight hours than Norman did in twenty years. And bit by bit, I've come to see what I did and what I was really part of. Maybe that's not enough, maybe it's just a fucking insult to the dead. But that's all I can give back to the world.

Pause.

John   Is it?

Pause.

This journey has always been about you.

Pause.

Don't ask me to forgive you. I can never do that.

Marius   I know.

Pause.

John   I'm not a religious man.

Marius   He was.

Pause.

John   Who?

Marius   Your father. Arguments with the commies in the movement. They came from different places. Am I right?

John   Very good. You did some research. Again. He lost belief. He said to me once: 'The God of prayer and faith is the God who presided over the slave trade, Holocaust and Rwandan genocide. We forgive him too easily.'

Pause.

Marius   I'm glad I saw you.

Pause.

And again, I'm sorry for what happened in your home. I'm sorry for everything.

Pause.

Another seat's come free.

Marius *stands.*

You know what it is today? Twenty-five years since I met you. To the day.

Pause.

If the old guy in the sky doesn't exist someone's got a strange fucking sense of humour.

John   There's something you need to know. In nineteen-eighty-eight, the year you cut off the head of your victim, another man was in Angola. Teaching politics to comrades. And he often came close to capture. The 'gook' you always refer to, could easily have been him.

On screen: **George Josana** *in Angola talking to a group of men.*

John   That man was my father.

Marius *tries to speak – but can't.*

John   What you do with the past, with your actions, that's all up to you. You need to make a reckoning with that, and it must be more than just talk.

Pause.

What you really want, Mr. Muller, I can never give you. Nor can any priest. Or shrink. Or Commission of Truth. In the end, we both know, that the man you must really talk to, is the man in the bush.

Blackout.

Scene Eight

Spot on **John**.

John   My father fought for a just world. Sacrificed a country and a wife and a home to do it. Yet he often said to me, 'The face of poverty is not only black.' But where he came from, it was. And everywhere else, mostly, it is.

Pause.

Apartheid is over in name. In law. But the idea behind it, the willingness, the fear, the madness, that hasn't gone. – My father always said racism is an illness. Whoever the oppressor, whoever the victim. But that to fall ill, the host must be willing. Welcoming. Joyous with their poison.

Pause.

This thing of – 'race'. Of how we are seen. How perceived. This needless burden that has plagued and ruined, shaped life and discourse for so long. That has determined how people live. Where they live. Who they marry. How they think. What they worship. How they hate.

Pause.

If they survive.

Pause.

And it's still there. The hate. It's in a gesture. An unconscious thought. A sidestep on a curb. An unwritten rule. An iron-clad law. And yes, down the barrel of a gun. It's in collusion. And most potent of all it's in silence. Silence that comes at you like a thunderclap.

Pause.

All the plays and books and films and poems and decrees it's fed. All the lives lost. Wasted. At the hands of pigs. Pigs, sick with delusion: George Floyd, Steve Biko, Stephen Lawrence, these are the people you know about. But there are millions more. And the eggshells we tread on conceal a problem we just can't seem to address. We wrap it in rules and laws and social contracts. And still real change never comes. King and Mandela are long dead. And the haters are still there. Everywhere. Rejoicing in their new world. Whipping through cyberspace, dispensing their venom.

Pause.

But history is in us. Around us. All. It's inescapable. And it's something we share on this tiny, delicate planet.

Pause.

My father. What would he make of it all now?

Pause.

Talk gets us nowhere, it seems. So: it's good to know the baseball bat's still in the cupboard.

Pause.

He was a great man. And citizen. And activist. Fearless and smart and tough. Wanting as a father. And a husband. But hell – if we're talking in religious terms, he's certainly a man I can forgive.

Pause.

Then there's the Afrikaner.

Pause.

After he came to my home, I met my mother.

On screen: **John**, *Orla,* **John**'s *mother,* **Joy**, *and her three grandchildren, in front of a rural African setting.*

John   I went back. Finally.

Pause.

I could see the wonder of the place. Could feel it. In the mountains. The scrub. That wild sea. And in the chaos, I saw glory. In the people. With a will to survive I know I'll never see again.

Pause.

She was older than I expected. Frail. And I was forced to look at a few things in myself. And in my father. He'd hardly talked of her. Did what she did because she was young, he said. But I sensed what he felt. That she couldn't commit enough to the struggle. I knew he still loved her. She gave me letters between them. Letters that lasted long after we'd fled. Letters I didn't know about. It painted another picture of her and made me think about him.

Pause.

His life was a crusade, but it put those close to him down the line. Without people like my father, change never comes. With them, family, as we know it, is out of the question. But at some point, we need to cut the cord with our parents. No matter how heroic they were. Or cruel. I think he understood that.

Pause.

For him, it was the fluttering of wings. For me . . .

He struggles for a moment.

It was going home. After so long. To a place I've so often written about. A place that denied me a mother and sent me on a childhood spinning through offices and meeting rooms and train stations in strange countries with my distracted father. That crushed millions beneath its boot. That cast such a long shadow over my life it took me fifty years to return. But in the end, I did. And he would have wanted that.

Pause.

And fuck me, if nothing else, that was down to Marius Muller.

Pause.

I can never offer him forgiveness. I don't have that power. I don't have that right. And anyway, I'm not God. But like absolution and atonement they're medieval get-outs. Cooked up by lonely men inside cold stone walls – so we can go on and on and never face justice.

Pause.

But in a way, maybe he has – a tortured kind of justice brought on by the life he chose to live since his war.

Pause.

He asked one final thing of me after our second meeting on the train. And he asked by letter. That this could happen. So the world, so you, could listen. This . . . phantom of a man, dared me to make it happen.

Spot on **Marius**, *watching* **John**.

John   And I agreed. – With a heavy heart.

Pause.

I had conditions. We'd never meet. We'd never share a platform again. It would be the last time we saw each other. And we'd never refer to what has happened in any way. Ever.

Pause.

Our 'vow of silence'.

Pause.

My sense has been that what was between us can never, should never, make sense. What I know or think I now know as a fifty-two-year-old man, is that certain things need to remain . . . inexplicable. Call me what you like, but he's been the man from the burning bus for twenty-five years. And I think that's enough.

Pause.

All I can say is this: two people met on train and had a chat. Something came of it.

John *turns to* **Marius**. *They stay locked on one another for a moment.*

John   What it was, who can say. But it happened.

John *turns back to us.*

Like now.

Flutter of tiny wings, growing louder.

Now you know.

The fluttering reaches a crescendo.

Blackout.

Zulu and Afrikaans words, meaning and pronunciation guide

(For an exact phonetic guide and German words please use an online dictionary which offers voiced pronunciations.)

Word	Meaning	Pronunciation
Apartheid	An oppressive system of legalised racial segregation in which targeted racial groups are deprived of political and civil rights.	Apart-ate
Fok weg	Fuck off	Fok as in *hawk* (short vowel); weg as in ve⟨ɦ⟩ i.e. a voiced glottal fricative. The 'e' as in *leg*.
Jusses	Jesus	Yu-siss. Yu as is *up*.
Kamieskroon	Rural village in SA	Cummees-crew-en. The 'r' can be trilled.
Pondoks	Hut	Pawnndorks (shorter vowel sound for both syllables)
Gat	Arsehole	Gut. The gu is ⟨ɦ⟩ i.e. a voiced glottal fricative. The 'u' as in *hut*.
Laaitie	A youth / young person	Lie-tea.
Klaared out	Discharged from army	Klaar as in *car*
Kak	Shit	Cuck
Spoeging	Spitting	Spoe⟨ɦ⟩ing. Spoe as in *put*; ging as in ⟨ɦ⟩*ing*; i.e. the first 'g' is a voiced glottal fricative.

Word	Meaning	Pronunciation
Klonkie	Offensive word for little black kid	Clawng-ki. The first vowel is shortened; the 'kie' as in *kick*.
Kippie	Name	Ki-pi as in *hippy*
Doef	Thud (slang)	Doef – vowel as in *cook*
Josana	African surname	Joe-zar-nuh. The 'uh' a short vowel.
Boer	Farmer / Afrikaner	Boo-er. The 'r' can be trilled.
Robey Leibrandt	Afrikaans boxer and Nazi	Robey as in *Row-bee*. brunt. The 'r' can be trilled.
Jan Smuts	Former SA president	Yun Smuts
Jy patetiese klein kak, jy sal slim word as dit die laaste ding wat ek doen om 'n paar brein in jou te klop!	You pathetic little shit, you will become smart if it's the last thing I do to beat some brains into you!	Yay, par-tear-tiss-er klane cuck, yay sull slerm (short vowel) vawrt (trill the 'r'), uss dit (as in *dert* – short vowel) dee larste derng (short vowel) vut ek (as in *heck*) doen (as in *put*) awm (short vowel) ern short vowel par (trill the 'r') brain (trill the 'r') ern yow (as in *no*) ter (short vowel) klawp! (short vowel).
Piet	Peter	Piet as in *hit*.
Dui! Afdeling aandag	Hey! Squad attention	Der-ee (both vowels short). Uff-dee-er-lerng. (short vowels) Arn-du⟨ɦ⟩ – i.e. a voiced glottal fricative.
Roofies	Recruits	Rewer-feese; trill the 'r'
Blougatte	Blue arses	Blow- ⟨ɦ⟩utter – i.e. a voiced glottal fricative.

Word	Meaning	Pronunciation
Oumanne	Old men	Owe-munner
Op die plek rus	Stand at ease	Awp (short vowel) di (as in *me*) pleck rurss (short vowel)
Parabats	Parachute brigade similar to SAS	Pa-rer-bats (the pa as in *hat*)
Bosbefok	Bushfucked	Borse (short vowel) burr forked (short vowel) fork (short vowel) bosbefok
Gook	SADF slang for freedom fighter	Gook (long vowel)
Shu (slang)	Wow	Shoe (short vowel as in *put*)
Sobukwe	Robert Sobukwe; former leader of the then banned Pan African Congress	Sir-book-wear (short vowel)
Sisulu	Walter Sisulu, former senior member of the ANC.	See-soo-loo
Ramphele	Mamphela Ramphele, anti-Apartheid activist	Rum-fair-lair
Gat kruiper	Arse creeper	Gat (see above) kray-per
Het jy my so fokkin Fyn?	Do you fucking understand me?	Het yay may soo-er (short vowels) fawkern (short vowels) fane?
Flukse fokkin bliksem	Clever fucking bastard	Flerksir (short vowels) fawkern (short vowels) blerkserm (short vowels)
Boet	Brother	Boet as in *put*.
Kief	Cool	As in *kick*. Kiff.
Sjambock	Leather whip	Sham-bock

Word	Meaning	Pronunciation
Hamba la!	Bugger off! (Zulu)	Hum-buh luh! (short vowels)
Nenga	River in the Transkei	Neng-guh
Transkei	Region of SA	Trarns-kigh
Ithemba	Hope	Ee-tem-buh (short vowels)
Befok	Fucked up	Burr-fork (short vowels)